Trucks
and
Cars

This book belongs to:

_____

Trucks
and
Cars

p

This is a Parragon Publishing Book.
This edition published in 2003

Illustrated by Mike Lacey,
Dud Moseley (SGA),
and Peter Wilks (SGA)
Edited by Caroline Repchuk
Designed by Kilnwood Graphics

Contents

The Beetle   6
Sports Cars   7
Racing Cars   8
Racing Trucks   9
Rally Cars   10
Pickup Racer   11
Hot Rods   12
Dragster   13
Early Cars   14
Family Cars   15
Stretch Limo   16
Luxury Cars   17
Ambulance   18
Fire Truck   19
Articulated Truck   20
Transporter   21
Army Trucks   22
Monster Trucks   24
Customized Trucks   25
Biggest Truck   26
Forklift Truck   27
Logger   28
Garbage Truck   29
Freezer Truck   30
Gas Tanker   30
Container Truck   31

The Beetle

The first Volkswagen was nicknamed the 'Beetle' because it looked a bit like a bug.

 # Sports Cars

Sports cars are usually much faster than ordinary cars, and their owners drive them for fun!

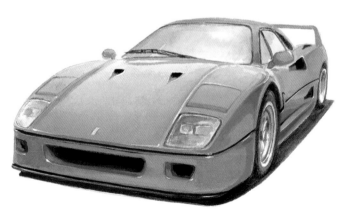

Racing Cars

Racing cars reach such high speeds that they need huge fins to stop them from taking off!

Racing Trucks

Trucks race in bumpy cross-country
rallies as well as around tracks.

Rally Cars

Family cars are given extra-powerful engines for off-road racing. Drivers wear crash helmets and safety harnesses.

Pickup Racer

Small trucks are adapted and given extra-powerful engines for racing.

Hot Rods

Old family cars are given huge tyres, an extra-powerful engine and are painted with colorful designs, to be raced all over the world.

Dragster

Dragsters race
at such great
speeds, they need
a parachute to
slow them down!

Early Cars

Early cars were started with a handle which you wound at the front. They had levers to steer with instead of a wheel, and they often used to break down.

Family Cars

We have always driven big family cars as American roads are wide and gas is cheap.

Stretch Limo

Limousines can be stretched, so that they are as long as a train.

The longest limousine in the world has 26 wheels, a swimming pool, a bed, and a helicopter landing pad!

Luxury Cars

Rolls Royces have always been luxurious and expensive. Their owners often have a chauffeur to drive them.

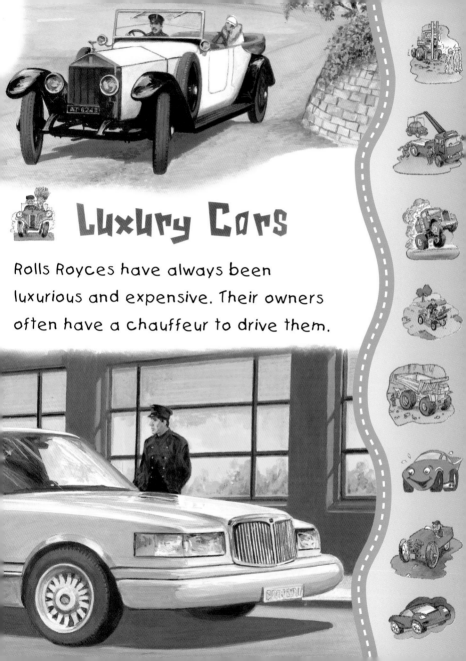

Ambulance

Ambulances take sick or injured people to hospital quickly.

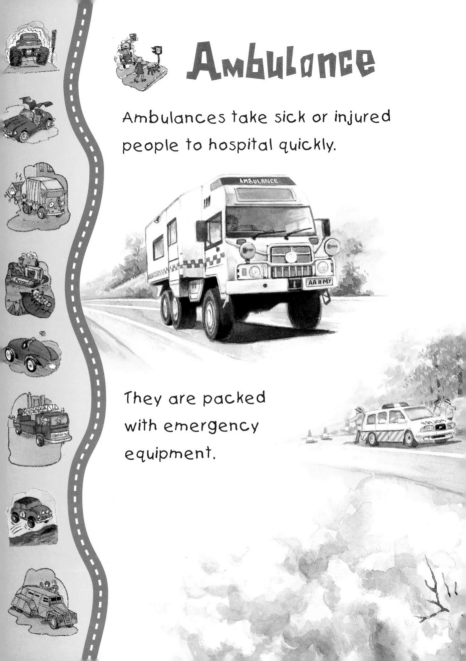

They are packed with emergency equipment.

Fire Truck

Fire trucks race to put out fires, and are full of hoses, medical equipment, axes for breaking down doors and ladders to reach fires in tall buildings.

Articulated Truck

Articulated trucks pull long trailers and they bend in the middle, so they can turn around corners.

 # Transporter

Transporters carry up to ten cars, all strapped down so they don't roll off! New trucks are sometimes delivered by being towed behind another truck.

Army Trucks

Some army trucks are covered in strong
metal armor plating to protect them.
They often have caterpillar tracks which

are bumpy strips of metal or rubber that wrap around their wheels. These stop their wheels getting stuck in sand or mud. Some trucks are tightly sealed so they can travel through shallow water.

Monster Trucks

Monster trucks are small pickup trucks that have been given huge dumper-truck wheels. They take part in races and drive over other cars, crushing them with their monster wheels!

Customized Trucks

Truckers sometimes paint their trucks with bright colors and pictures, add extra lights, or shiny metal bodywork — just to make them look different, and stand out from the crowd!

 # Biggest Truck

The world's biggest truck is a dump truck called the Terex Titan. Each wheel is twice as high as a person and weighs as much as three family cars!

It is too big to travel on the road, and has to be taken to pieces and carried on a transporter!

Forklift Truck

These trucks
slide their forks
under wooden
pallets to pick
up heavy loads
and move
them around
factories.

 # Logger

Logs are much too heavy to be put on a truck by hand, so a Logger is used.

Loggers have a special crane that picks up logs and loads the truck to take logs from the forest to the factory.

 # Garbage Truck

Garbage trucks have special crushers that squash the garbage up, before emptying it at the dump.

Freezer Truck

This truck is like a big freezer on wheels. It is used to deliver frozen food.

Gas Tanker

Gas tankers can deliver enough gas to gas stations to fill up 500 cars.

Container Truck

Container trucks collect containers of goods from big ships, and deliver them to the shops.